STOCK SCREENER CRITERIA

THE WORLD'S MOST BORING, YET RELIABLE, OPTIONS STRATEGY

Trading Academy

TABLE OF CONTENTS

INTRODUCTION 6

Chapter 1: THE WORLD'S MOST BORING, YET RELIABLE, OPTIONS STRATEGY 13

Who Is This for?..17

Why Do Some Sources Claim You Can Earn 100% Annual Returns?..20

Chapter 2 HOW THE WHEEL WORKS – STEP BY STEP..........24

Figure 1: A visual overview of the different stages of The Wheel Strategy..25

STEP ONE: CHOOSE A STOCK 26

STEP TWO: SELLING CASH-SECURED PUTS 27

Expiration and Assignment..30

STEP THREE: AFTER THE CSP EXPIRES 33

STEP FOUR: SELL A COVERED CALL 34

Scenario One..35

Scenario Two..37

Managing a Covered Call..39

MAKING THE WHEEL TURN 42

Chapter 3 CHOOSING A BROKER 46

Trading Commissions and Fees..46

SOFTWARE..48

CUSTOMER SERVICE QUALITY..51

OPTIONS ACCOUNT LEVEL REQUIREMENTS........................53

FEE SCHEDULE..54

TWO BROKERS WE RECOMMEND FOR THE WHEEL STRATEGY 56

Tastyworks by Tastytrade..56

Thinkorswim by TD Ameritrade 56

"CAN I USE ROBINHOOD OR WEBULL FOR THIS?" 57

Chapter 4 CHOOSING THE RIGHT CANDIDATES 58

Selection Criteria 60

Trend Characteristics 60

Stock Price 63

Stock Category 65

No IPOs 66

Stick to Boring Companies 67

No Media Darlings 72

No Penny Stocks 75

Specialty ETFs 77

    STOCK SCREENER CRITERIA 82

Optionality 82

Price 82

Volume 83

Stability 83

Bullish Trend 84

No Upcoming Events 84

Paid Screening Tools 86

INTRODUCTION

The stock market has always attracted people who are looking to get rich. Speculative forces in the market have dictated short-term price moves for over a century now, and it's unfortunate that all stock market activity is often painted as one large speculative play. New entrants to the marketthink all they need to do to make money is buy when a stock will go up and then exit before it goes down. However, reality soon sets in once they put their money on the line.

Our answer to the "How do I make money in stocks?" question has always been the same. The best method is a long-term buy and hold strategy in which you behave like an investor in a business. Dividends can supercharge your returns in that time period while alternative assets like gold and cryptocurrencies will hedge your portfolio against inflation and any untoward occurrences with the US dollar.

So where do options fall into this? Options are often highlighted as examples of speculative financial instruments. Most intelligent investors, we're told, stay away from them for fear they can go wrong in a hurry. This is true. However, we'd like to point out that options go wrong when you don't understand how they work, or their intended strategies. You can make options as complex as possible or you can use them in simple, reliable ways.

One of the qualities that makes options trading so enticing is the ability to generate income. For the longest time, bonds and dividend stocks were viewed as the only safe sources of income, but this isn't true. Options, when used in a sound strategy, have the ability to make you just as much money, if not more, than dividends. And the strategy we present in this book can enable you to earn that money with a much smaller base of capital.

Executing such strategies requires a lot of patience and a willingness to slowly compound your money. This approach is opposed to the often advertised "collect 200%+ returns every year" day trading methods that will have you running huge risks with your capital. In our view, minimizing risk is far more important than shooting for huge gains.

In the professional money management world, risk-adjusted gains matter more than absolute returns. After all, anyone can generate 100% returns if they're risking 150% per trade! Generating 15-20% returns while risking just one percent or less of your capital is far tougher. Adopting a lower risk approach ensures you won't lose money when you do lose, which is the firststep to making long term gains.

The strategy we're going to explain in this book, called The Wheel, is a simple one that uses options conservatively. You're going to learn how to construct a portfolio that will generate anywhere between 15-25% per year in additional income. If your aim is to generate 100% or some astronomical figure on your capital, we're sorry to say that we can't help you with that.

Our strategy is low risk, and some would even say boring. Don't mistake this to mean it's ineffective. When it comes to the stock market, boringbeats exciting. In fact, if you've traded options before, you'll recognize many of the terms and components of The Wheel.

However, the true power of our strategy lies in its ability to generate income consistently, without having you absorb additional risk. There are very few strategies that can make similar claims. Consistency and scalability areimportant for every investment strategy and the Wheel checks both boxes. Although it works whether you have just $1,000 in your account or $1 million.

We recommend that you have a basic portfolio in place before implementing The Wheel. We're doing this to reduce your risk even further and ensure you'll always have some portion of your money bringing you returns no matter what. While The Wheel is a great strategy to make money, it's best to use it within a larger risk-minimized framework.

The Wheel uses options and it's understandable if you have objections to trading them. Many long-term investors have been scared away from options by the uninformed financial media. You've been led to think they'redoomsday devices. However, the truth is far more subtle. Options are merely tools. Just as a knife can be used to cause harm or used for good, options can be used in the wrong ways to cause staggering losses.

There have been many instances of famous investors using options to boost their gains or even construct entire portfolios from them. Let's start with the biggest of them all, Warren Buffett. He has been quoted as calling derivatives "financial WMDs" in the past, so you'd think he'd stay well away from options. However, he routinely buys and sells puts to generate income for Berkshire Hathaway. It isn't a strategy he uses very often, but if he's carrying large amounts of cash, he puts it to work by selling puts and collecting premiums.

Buffett is an example of someone who conservatively uses options. On the other end of the spectrum, the 2008 financial crisis saw Jamie Mai and Charlie Ledley of Cornwall Capital turn $110,000 into $136 million before they went on to call the top of the American housing market. Their feats were detailed in Michael Lewis's book *The Big Short*. Mai and Ledley used options to build their capital by placing bets on asymmetric opportunities, where the reward was far greater than the risk. Options trades can bedesigned to reward such situations, and they made the most of it.

The author is a well-known name to anyone who has played blackjack. The author of *Beat the Dealer* was also a prolific options trader who averaged 20% per year over a 30-year period trading options.

And perhaps the best example of an options trade was made outside the financial markets by George Lucas (Artemis Capital Management LP, 2016). The creator of *Star Wars* famously chose to forego his $750,000 director's fee in exchange for the rights to merchandising, sequels, and licensing the *Star Wars* franchise. The rest is history, and Lucas cashed his rights in when Disney bought the franchise for $4 billion in 2015. Deciding to buy the rights instead of cash is an options trade, in essence.

We're not claiming you can turn nothing into $4 billion by reading this book. In fact, we're cautioning against thinking like this. However, we can assure you that the strategy in this book has the potential to make you an additional 15-25% per year without additional risk to your portfolio. It will augment whatever income you already collect on your stock holdings.

You don't need massive capital or special expertise. It's best if you're familiar with the stock market and further understand how options work. After all, it's tough to implement an options trading strategy if you don't understand what a call or a put is. We'll have you shorting options in this book, so you will need to understand the implications of that.

You'll also need to know your broker requirements for options trading approval. This book will help you with that.

Lastly, we ask that you exercise a lot of patience when learning this strategy. It might be simple, but don't confuse this for being easy. Although the technical aspects of this strategy aren't tough, executing it with patience and discipline is. It takes time for The Wheel to truly produce fruits and you need to be willing to give it time to grow.

You'll find that you can use The Wheel strategy on just about any investment vehicle that is optionable. Throughout this book, we'll often refer to "stocks", but know that we mean the broader array of financial instruments that includes ETFs and other Exchange Traded Products. We'll also talk of "trades" or trading. By no means are we implying day trading or any time frame with those terms. We are simply referring to a transaction conducted on a securities exchange.

So having said all that, let's move forward and take a look at what The Wheel is and how it works.

Chapter 1 :
THE WORLD'S MOST BORING, YET RELIABLE, OPTIONS STRATEGY

So what is The Wheel Strategy, and why is it so powerful? To begin with, you're not going to experience the stereotypical rollercoaster of emotions that many investors associate with options. In fact, the Wheel is a straightforward strategy that anyone can execute with just an additional two or three hours per week to dedicate to a portfolio.

With the wheel, you can expect safe and continuous gains no matter the volatility or unpredictability in the stock market. What's more, the gains you can earn will outpace traditional dividend investing. Currently the average dividend yield on an S&P 500 stock is just 1.48%, with the average yield for a Dividend Aristocrat stock just 3.5%. The Wheel can generate annual returns far greater than that, without additional risk.

The Wheel is also referred to as the Triple Income Strategy or "Buy and Hold on Steroids." This is because there are three income components in the strategy.

Income #1 - You collect the premium from selling cash-secured puts

Income #2 - You collect the premium from selling covered calls Income #3 - You collect cash when your covered call gets assigned and you sell your shares

As you can see, The Wheel requires you to sell cash-covered puts (CSPs) and write covered calls (CCs). Let's examine these in more detail.

EXPLORING THE WHEEL

To understand The Wheel, you need to fully understand what cash-secured puts and covered calls are.

The cash-secured put (CSP) is a great way to get paid to enter a trade. Here's how it works. Let's say you wish to own a stock but would like to generate additional cash upon entry. You sell (write) a put that is exercisable at a print that is close to the price at which you would like to pay to buy the stock. Because you are selling an option, you collect a payment, called the premium. Because the put is close to the money (meaning close to the current market price of the stock), the premium will be significant. If the put finishes in the money (ITM), you'll be required to buy the stock.

This is fine because you originally wanted to own the stock. However, if the put finishes at a price that makes it worthless, referred to as out of the money (OTM), you can repeat the process - write another CSP and collect a premium once again. Eventually you will be buying the stock, and then be able to wait for your investment to mature. However, cash-secured puts area great way to boost your investment returns in advance of that purchase.

Once you own the stock, you can begin to sell covered calls (CC). A CC isa two-part trade where you own the underlying stock and write a call against it, typically at an OTM strike price. Because you're writing an option, you'll collect the premium on it. If the option moves ITM at expiration, you will be "assigned" and have to sell your stock. (No problem

– just sell another put option on the same stock and repeat the process!) However, if you write the call at a price that is well outside the money upon the option's expiration, you get to keep your stock as well as the premium.

The CC can be used as a speculative strategy as well. You can buy a stock and write a call that is close to the money. If the price of the stock rises to ensure the option finishes ITM, you get to keep the premium and sell the underlying stock for a profit. It's hard to make this speculative strategywork over the long term because you can't predict market moves, but the covered call can be a great way to earn additional gains on existing portfolio holdings.

In essence, CSPs pay you to buy shares you like,

while CCs can pay you to sell shares that you wish to sell. Trading like this isn't sexy or exciting.Over the course of a year, this approach can translate into a significant addition to your cash reserves. Over five years or a decade, the returns will add up significantly, especially when you take compounding into account.

Earning a 20% return depends on stock selection, your experience, andmost of all, your willingness to stay the course and patiently execute your strategies. It's pretty boring but it passes the ultimate test, in our eyes. You'll be able to sleep well at night.

Who Is This for?

The Wheel is for anybody who wants to boost returns and earn additional cash on an existing portfolio. Retirees or those who are income-oriented in their portfolio will benefit massively from this strategy. You can collect additional income on top of your dividends. While the returns might vary, depending on the makeup of your portfolio, you can rest assured that it is a consistent stream of income when you follow the steps and advice wedescribe in this book.

We've always said that options should be used as an additional to your core portfolio, not as a substitution. The Wheel is no different and is best used by people who have a base portfolio in place.

Here's a sample portfolio allocation for retirement:

40% of your portfolio in *Dividend Growth Investing* stocks/ETFs/Closed End Funds (CEFs) 25% in bonds
15% dedicated to The Wheel
10% in higher growth stocks with no dividend payment 5% gold
5% crypto

If you are young and just beginning to build a portfolio, you might allocate funds with these percentages:

25% in *Dividend Growth Investing* stocks/funds/Closed End Funds 15% dedicated to The Wheel
50% in higher growth stocks with no dividend payment 5% gold
5% crypto

These percentages will vary depending on your investment goals, but we recommend assigning a small portion of your portfolio to The Wheel. We've noted 15% for those with an existing portfolio, but it can be as high as 25% if income is your primary goal. A huge benefit of The Wheel, particularly for those just beginning to builda portfolio, is that it can lower your cost basis of stock ownership – rather than buying shares outright, you sell puts and acquire the shares through assignment. Over the long term, you could effectively end up owning your favorite stock for free, by continuing to sell puts and calls.

Note that this strategy isn't a magic bullet. It isn't something you can generate astronomical returns with, especially if you don't have lots of capital. For example, to execute The Wheel on Amazon stock, your broker would require you to have $340,000 in your account just to sell cash-secured puts.

We would also like to point out that every investment strategy does have risks attached to it. The Wheel has previously been termed a covered call on steroids. This description makes it seem as if you can attain all the benefits of the covered call without adding additional risk. While The Wheel does not require you to absorb high levels of risk, it is incorrect to say that there is zero risk.

The Wheel isn't going to give you free money, as beginners often say when they talk about covered calls. There is no such thing as free money. The CSP and CC don't add any risk to your position, and this is why it can seem as if you're earning "free" money. However, the risk of your stock dropping to zero is still a substantial risk that you undertake whenever you commit money in the financial markets.

Why Do Some Sources Claim You Can Earn 100% Annual Returns?

Read about The Wheel Strategy online and you'll come across promises of earning 100% or more returns on your money each and every year. These claims seem very credible because many provide a spreadsheet for you to plug in numbers and project returns. However, once you try to execute the strategy, you'll realize that earning these kinds of returns is a hit-or-miss prospect.

These spreadsheets assume you'll write options on stocks that have high implied volatility (IV) levels, and therefore high premiums. While high-IV stocks have a great chance of behaving the way you want them to, they're just as likely to behave in the opposite manner. The high IV tells you that the stock's price is likely to have wide swings. This means you're never going to be sure how your trades are going to end up.

Over the course of a year, you'll find that many of these kinds of trades willgo against you, and as a result, achieving 100% returns is pretty much impossible. Of course, this is before we even explore the mental stress such a high risk-to-reward strategy will cause. Instead of aiming for such high returns, it's far better to set your sights lower and collect a decent, more consistent, return on your money.

You will read posts on online forums about how some people claim to be earning 20% per month using The Wheel. Look closer, though, and you'll notice that all of them have been running the strategy for a few months at best, and often in extremely bullish market conditions. In the long run, it's impossible to generate such astronomical returns without risking an unacceptable amount of capital. Do not let these profit claims pull you astray. Stick to the plan we set out for you, and you will do better in thelong run.

We're not saying 100% per year is unattainable as a one-off in certain market circumstances. It's just that it's highly unlikely for anyone to consistently achieve these kinds of returns over a decade or longer.

A more realistic number for you to target is 0.3-0.5% per week. This will give you an annualized return between 15-26%. These returns, when compounded over a number of years, are significantly higher than what the average market participant earns.

A market-tracking ETF earns around 9% per year. Even if you earn 15%per year, you're getting more than 150% of what the market gives you routinely. The other thing to remember is that The Wheel works whether themarket is bullish, bearish, or neutral. The cash flow you earn during bear markets will boost your overall return immeasurably and will offset the unrealized capital losses in your portfolio.

To drill our point home, we'd like to use a baseball analogy. Let other market participants aim for home runs all the time. It's far better for you to concentrate on hitting singles and doubles consistently.

Now that we have set expectations in place, let's move forward and look athow The Wheel works.

Chapter 2
HOW THE WHEEL
WORKS – STEP BY STEP

Experienced options traders will appreciate the simplicity of The Wheel. Sowhy don't more options traders use this approach? The simple answer is that it is a rather unsexy strategy. Professional options traders, who have theentire day to devote to the market, don't find it attractive to spend just two to three hours per week on The Wheel.

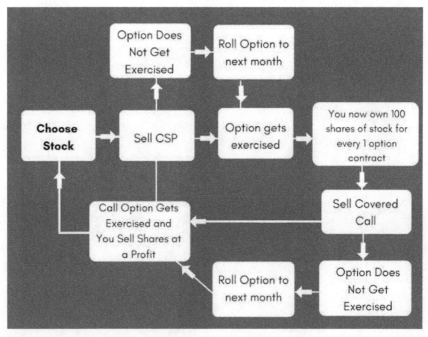

Figure 1: A visual overview of the different stages of The Wheel Strategy

The Wheel is best suited for those who don't have time to monitor the markets closely and want a conservative way of earning a decent return. The way The Wheel enables this is through a multi-step process. As you can see from the diagram, the process can circle around and around, like a wheel, allowing you to earn options premiums again and again

Let's break down each step and see how it works.

STEP ONE: CHOOSE A STOCK

The first step is choosing a stock. This should be one you have researched and are comfortable with its long-term growth prospects. See our books, The 8 Step Beginner's Guide To Value Investing and Dividend Growth Investing for guidance on selecting quality stocks. To filter for stocks which work best for the wheel strategy, we cover this in depth inside chapter 4 of this book.

To implement The Wheel strategy, you will need a company with listed options. That may sound obvious, but not every stock has an active options market. Recent IPOs, for example, are not viable choices.

STEP TWO: SELLING CASH-SECURED PUTS

When you sell (write) a put, you are taking on the obligation to buy at a particular price, called the strike. Every time a put is sold, someone is onthe other side of the transaction, taking a "long" put position. Long putsgive a person the right to sell stock at the strike price, maybe even beforethe expiration date. By writing a put, then, you are entering into a contract where you must buy the stock for the strike price if it expires ITM, or if the holder of the long position decides "to put it to you". The holder of the longside pays the premium that you get to keep, no matter what price the stock may reach when the put either expires or is assigned to you.

Let's look at an example with AT&T. At the time of this writing, the stock was trading at $28.77. Let's assume you have no qualms about owning it at this price. You think its long-term prospects are great and therefore you write a put with a strike price of $28.50, which is the closest ITM strike on AT&T's option chain.

Remember, writing a put means you will have to buy the stock at the strike

-- $28.50 -- if the long put holder exercises the option. Let's assume the current price for your put is $0.60 per contract and it will expire in 30 days. (One contract will obligate you to buy 100 shares if the put is exercised.) Therefore $60 will be deposited into your account straight away ($0.60 * 100)

Here's where the "cash" portion of the strategy enters. Because you're writing puts, your broker is going to limit your risk exposure and require you to have cash in hand to buy AT&T in case it finishes ITM – at or belowthe $28.50. This means you'll need to have enough cash to buy 100 shares of AT&T (if you wrote one put; if you wrote two puts, you'll need cash for 200 shares).

Your put's strike price is $28.50, so you'll need $2,850 as cash in your account to execute one CSP on AT&T. This may seem like a pretty large amount to have just sitting in cash, but it is enabling you to carry out this strategy. This is why we mentioned earlier that it's best to use The Wheel asa secondary income generation strategy and not a primary one.

If you like AT&T's long term prospects, but don't have the money to buy 100 shares, , then you must decide if you want to simply buy some shares now, or wait until you have the cash.

However, waiting has an opportunity cost. Let's say it takes you a year to gather $2,850, but during that time, AT&T's stock price has rocketed 50% higher. Now you'll need $4,275 to write a CSP! If you've done proper research into a stock, and believe it to be a good investment, you will probably do better buying as many shares as you can afford, rather than waiting.

Using the number in our example, if you have the $2,850 in your account, you'll earn $60 for the CSP in a month (remember we said we assume the put expires in 30 days). That's 2.1% or around 25% annualized. Compare this to the 50% potential capital gain you've left on the table and you'll see that waiting is a poor choice, from an opportunity cost perspective. Later in this book we'll be going into the minimum acceptable strike price for both your CSP and CC to make executing The Wheel worth your time.

If you don't have the money to write a CSP on a given stock, buy the stock as best as you can and then search for other CSP candidates. The cash return you'll earn from a CSP will always pale compared to the capitalgains you'll receive from a long-term investment holding.

If you don't have the money to write a CSP on a given stock, then you mustdecide how committed you are to the long-term prospects of the company. Do you buy a few shares now, or do you wait? Other opportunities can always be found, and you can search for them while you are building your cash reserves. You must remember though, that the cash percentage return you'll earn with The Wheel strategy pale compared to the capital gains you'll receive from a long-term investment holding.

Expiration and Assignment

Let's assume you do have the cash that your broker requires, and you have written a CSP. All options expire at some point in time, and there are two possible results. The first is that the option finishes OTM and the second is that the option finishes ITM. (An ATM finish is treated the same as an ITMone.)

Let's examine what happens in the first case.

If the CSP option finishes OTM, meaning the stock's market price is greaterthan the put's strike price, you get to keep the premium and your cash balance remains intact. You won't have the option assigned to you. This leaves you free to write another CSP and ride it to expiration (also called expiry). With this strategy as with most written options, it's frequently best to pick an expiration that is between 21-45 days away. We'll discuss the reasons in detail later in this book. For now, understand that when you write an option, you are selling time, and the more time until the expiration date, the more you should be paid.

This plan means every CSP you write will last for around a month. Some traders write options that expire in only a week for high-IV stocks. High-IV stocks have larger premiums attached to their options and this makes up for the lack of time decay on a weekly option. Unless you want to spend a lot of time monitoring the trade, we recommend that you stick to the 21-45 days.

Now that you have a CSP, you have the risk is that the option finishes ITM (or ATM). So, what happens in this scenario?

Your broker will assign you the option, which means you'll have to buy the stock at the strike price. Because you have the cash necessary to cover this purchase, buying the stock isn't an issue. A CSP is therefore a win-win for everyone involved. You get to own the stock that you're keen on, essentially at a lower price than what you would have paid had you bought the stock outright. If the stock price rises to a small extent and the option finishes OTM, you've earned a small premium on your investment and can write another CSP.

The only risk with the CSP is that the underlying stock rises by a huge extent. This means you'll have missed the capital gains in exchange for a small premium. This scenario often happens with highly volatile stocks. We'll later explain how you can screen out such risky stocks when implementing this strategy.

For now, you can see how the CSP is a great way to be bullish on a stock and get paid to enter a position. Note that the CSP is different from a cash covered put. A cash covered put is initialized when you already own the stock in question and write puts against it. A CSP "covers" you via the cash you hold in your account.

STEP THREE: AFTER THE CSP EXPIRES

Depending on where your CSP finishes, you'll either initiate a new CSP or buy the underlying stock. This step isn't very complicated and can be done with just the click of a button (brokers will automatically transact the stock purchase when you are assigned). Some traders move on from the original stock and initiate a new position in another stock. To us, this doesn't make much sense.

Remember that you should initiate CSPs only on stocks that you're keen on owning. Do not make the mistake of writing CSPs on random stocks because you think they won't finish ITM. This is a highly speculativestrategy that is not an intelligent way of investing. Follow the investment principles we outlined in our previous books and identify the stocks you would love to own. Execute CSPs on those stocks only.

Assuming your option finished ITM, you'll then move on to the next step ofthe strategy.

STEP FOUR: SELL A COVERED CALL

You now own the stock from the CSP finishing ITM, and are ready to write a covered call. The CC is a two-part trade. The primary, money-making leg is a long stock position, and the second leg is a short call. CCs can be used for both long-term investment as well as short-term income. For an in-depth discussion see our previous book, Covered Calls for Beginners.

Whether you plan to hold the stock long term or short term doesn't matter. All that matters is that you believe the stock has a good future and will trend upwards. Of course, that doesn't mean it needs to skyrocket immediately. In fact those kinds of stocks are not ideal covered call candidates . Instead we are looking for stocks with an overall mildly bullish trend to them.

Later you will read that we recommend "boring" companies for The Wheel. You don't want a stock that tends to move sharply on earnings – the unpredictability makes strike price selection very difficult. However, if yours is not boring and tends to move on earnings, it might be best to wait until after the announcement to write your call.

Also, many stocks see increased interest as the ex-dividend date approaches. Institutions, for example, use complex formulae to target dividend "grabs", where they buy a stock shortly before the ex-dividend date, become eligible to collect the dividend, and then sell the stock immediately afterwards. Before you write that call, then, make sure you've evaluated the stock's dividend schedule and price action patterns around important dates. Technical analysis of the stock can help, and we'll offer some guidance in Chapter 5.

Once you've decided on a strike price, you will also need to choose an expiration date. Remember, the more time you have the option open, the more you should get paid, but we recommend that you stay within that 21- 45 day window. If the call is assigned to you, you have stock ownership to "cover" it, hence the name.

Here are two scenarios that can play out in this trade.

Scenario One

The first scenario is the most negative one. Let's say your analysis was incorrect and the stock declines instead of rising. In this situation, your call remains OTM, and expires, with you keeping the premium collected, while your stock moves into a loss. However, this loss is offset by the premium you'll earn by writing the call. Here's what the math looks like:

Loss on the trade = Loss from long stock leg - Premium collected from short call

The closer your call was to the money when you wrote it, the greater the premium you stood to earn. If the stock's price decline is small, you may actually have a breakeven situation. You will still own the stock and therefore have the potential to sell another CC.

What happens if the stock loss is NOT small and it keeps declining?

You will need to decide what your conviction is -- if you are convinced that the downturn is temporary, you can continue to hold the stock and sell OTM CCs to collect the premiums. Of course, you'll need to select strike prices that don't risk ITM expirations if you want to keep the stock long term.

If you have lost interest in the stock and want to exit the stock position, you could choose to write the next CC ITM and have the stock called away from you.

If, however, your objective was simply to earn a short-term profit, this is a poor situation indeed. Some traders set stop loss orders at the breakeven point. By setting the order in advance, the broker should automatically sell the stock. Be careful, however, that such a situation doesn't leave you witha "naked" short call, where you no longer own the stock, but you still have the call obligation that you established when you sold the CC. You'll need to check with your broker to determine if the stop loss order will include thesale of the call along with the stock. Remember that each single option contract represents 100 shares. You will not be able to sell CCs if you own less than 100.

This means the covered call is best executed either on stocks you wouldlove to own for the long term and don't mind shelling out cash for, or on low-priced stocks that you believe are under-valued and have good appreciation potential in the short term.

Scenario Two

The second scenario occurs when the stock rises but not so much as tomove the call ITM. In this case, your CC will expire worthless and you can then write another CC. Ideally, your stock will rise slowly, steadily over time, and you'll write OTM CCs over and over, generating that extraincome. If you decide you no longer want to hold the stock, you'll want to sell by writing a CC with a strike price that will cause the call to beassigned. Thus, you'll earn a profit equal to the strike price (your stock exit price) minus the buying price plus the premium earned by writing the call.

Profit = (Sale price of long stock - Buy price of long stock) + Premium earned by writing call Choosing strike prices is not as easy as it sounds. How close should the strike be to your stock's current price? When you place your strike price farfrom your entry, you'll decrease your profits by doing so. On the flip side, you'll earn a higher premium by writing a call that's closer to the money, but risk having the stock called away. The best way to figure out where you ought to place your strike is to explore the options calculator on yourbroker's software. We'll explain how you can choose the best broker in the next chapter.

For now, understand that it's best to model various scenarios on the calculator to figure out the tradeoffs. For example, if the premium you can earn by writing a call closer to the money makes up for the potential gains you'll give up on the long stock, it's worth placing this trade. By minimizing the middle-of-the-road zone, you'll increase your chances of earning your maximum profit. Also remember: if your stock is called away, you can always buy it back!

Managing a Covered Call

There are a few ancillary fees to consider when it comes to the CC. Option assignment is an important factor when designing your strategy. Thanks to the way brokers operate, many traders actively shun assignment and this defines your maximum profit.

Brokers that charge assignment fees can eat into your profits massively. We don't mean to say that such brokers are bad or somehow inefficient. That would be too simplistic. You'll need to focus on the overall package that they offer. However, if you'll be paying assignment fees, check to see how much they'll reduce your profit. You might be better off writing calls that are well OTM, thereby avoiding assignment and fees. Of course, this means that the premium you collect will be smaller, but you will still enjoy the profits of stock's upward move.

Covered calls are an easy trade to manage, but that doesn't mean you can ignore them or your investments. It's your money and you should always pay attention to your portfolio. You'll need to pay particular attention as the expiration date approaches, because you'll be faced with decisions.

What if the call is ITM and you don't want to be assigned? You can always buy back the call. Or, you can "roll" the call by simultaneously buying it back and selling another at a different strike price or expiration date. Even ifthe call is OTM, you may want to roll it before expiration.

What if your stock has declined, and the call is now significantly OTM? In this scenario, you should buy back your call rather than wait for it to expire, and then write another call a few strikes below.

As with the CSP, you want to write options that are in that 21-45 day window discussed earlier. With every passing day, an option loses value, a concept called time decay, and that decay accelerates as the expiration date gets nearer. You should take full advantage of it.

Your decision to roll your strike prices should be

governed by your trade objectives and whether you can evaluate your reasons for entry. If you find that your stock analysis was incorrect, it's best to shut the trade down and evaluate the possibilities with an other stock.

If you want to own the stock for the long haul, then you need to be carefulto place your strikes at a good distance away from the current market price so that the stock isn't called away. You don't want to lose long-term price appreciation in exchange for an option premium. The premium will amount to just a few percentage points while the unrealized gains on the stock can be much higher.

MAKING THE WHEEL TURN

Now that you've learned about the CSP and the CC, how can you bring everything together to form The Wheel? For starters, both strategies produce income to a certain extent. However, when you combine the two together, you supercharge the money you can earn from your investment.

The trade begins with you selecting a stock, writing a CSP, and thenmonitoring how it works out. If the put moves ITM, you keep the premium and buy the stock. This opens the next step of the trade which is the CC. Now that you own the stock, you can sell CCs again and again, keeping the premiums you earn from writing the calls.

When viewed overall, you have two income-producing legs and one long stock leg that should bring you long-term unrealized capital gains. The income legs can add an additional 5 to 10% returns annually and this iswhat ensures you'll earn an average of 15-20% annually on your portfolio.

The key is to operate in stocks that you want to hold for the long term. While speculative strategies can work, it's best to stick to long-term investments because short-term trades require more monitoring and can be tough to replicate over the long term. We recommend running this strategy with options that have expiry dates a month out, but you can use weekly options as well.

Managing The Wheel is also straightforward when you've adopted a long- term investment approach. If you've properly researched the company, you don't have to worry about your approach to the long stock. You simply keep holding it unless your primary investment thesis turns out to be false. As for the strike prices of the CSP and CC, you can either roll them up or down depending on the way the market behaves.

If your CSP doesn't get assigned, you've profited from the transaction, and you can write another put that might be closer to the money. If the stock you're interested in is on a massive bull run, it's better to simply buy the stock outright instead of trying to acquire it with your CSP. However, such runs happen rarely and you can rest assured that for the most part, a CSP that's written close to the money will usually finish ITM.

Should you write puts that are far OTM? In our opinion, this doesn't make a lot of sense. Your objective with The Wheel should be to ultimately gain ownership of the stock. Writing a CSP that is far OTM doesn't achieve this. Long-term investors will benefit from pushing their calls OTM but not their puts.

To reiterate, here are the three streams of income you can earn with The Wheel:

Income #1 - you collect the premium from selling puts.

Income #2 - you collect the premium from selling covered calls. Income #3 - you collect the cash when your covered call gets assigned and you sell your shares.

The great thing about The Wheel is that you keep your premiums no matter what. It doesn't matter what happens to the long stock, you keep the premiums you receive from writing options. If the world were to come to an end and everyone sold everything, you'd still keep your premiums. Admittedly, you'd have bigger problems to worry about in that scenario, but it goes to show how certain option premiums are.

Aside from this, there's the obvious benefit that you

can earn two streamsof income on your investment instead of just one. Usually, investors implement covered calls to generate income, but if you have the cash to buy a stock and then sell a covered call, it makes sense to first put it to use witha CSP. You'll double the income you earn from your trade.

Chapter 3
CHOOSING A BROKER

As easy as it is to just run The Wheel using your regular broker, it's worth figuring out if there is a better option.

There are a few elements you need to consider before choosing an options broker. Let's look at them one by one.

Trading Commissions and Fees

Commissions and fees are a considerable headwind to overcome when it comes to trading. With options, there are government fees that are the same across all brokers, and then there are two tiers of commissions/fees that will vary from broker to broker. The first tier is the cost of buying and selling options. This cost is similar to the commissions you'll pay when buying or selling stocks. Most brokers will list per contract commissions, but some will have a model where you'll pay a fixed charge up to a certain level of trading activity, and then will pay on a different schedule when you trade above this threshold.

Thanks to the rise in discount brokers, there are many brokers who don't charge commissions to trade options contracts, but will charge fixed contract fees, which means you still end up paying to trade, but it might be just $0.50-$1 per options contract. That sounds like it could get expensive, but most brokers have a maximum price per trade. For example, the contract fees on Tastyworks are capped at $10 regardless of the trade size.

Not every broker will charge you contract fees, so this makes your choice a little more confusing. Take the time to consider your trading volume and look at the commissions and fees schedule that the broker advertises. At the very least, you should expect to pay no trading commissions because there are so many app-based firms that don't charge these.

In the second tier you might pay fees when a call or put is exercised or assigned. Once again, some brokers don't charge for this activity, so you need to consider this cost in your decision analysis. (Options buyers pay exercise fees. Assignment fees are what options sellers pay. It's the same fee, except the name changes depending on which side of the trade you've assumed.)

Add these commissions and fees together to take your final cost to trade into account. One broker might charge zero commissions but higher assignment fees. Remember that these fees eat away at your profits, so you need to be aware of them before trading.

As a rule of thumb, when you're just starting with 1-2 contracts per trade, if your total trade fees (opening/closing/exercise/assignment) add up to more than $15 per trade, you need to find another broker!

SOFTWARE

Broker trading platforms vary greatly. The best brokers to pick are the ones who cater exclusively to active traders. These companies have the most sophisticated tools. Having said that, the platforms that these brokers provide can be quite complex, so you don't want to choose one that requires you to go through a steep learning curve.

Avoid choosing brokers who cater to long-term investors. A tell-tale sign is a lack of services and platform features. Long-term investment is a different game entirely, and most investors don't need sophisticated charting tools or options visualization tools. In fact, many long-term investors don't even need or want a real-time chart.

This is not the case for options traders. You need tools to help you enter proposed strike prices, and you'll clearly be able to see your break even points and maximum profit and loss scenarios.

You don't need standalone desktop terminals to execute these strategies. You'll be spending perhaps a few hours every month maintaining these setups, so it's not as if you need a supercomputer to make them work. A web-based software is more than enough for your needs.

If your broker's charting interface is clunky, you need to find anotherbroker. The competition is keen for your business and serious brokers have elegant software for charting and options trading. If you are not ready to change brokers, then you can use a resource such as tradingview.com or stockcharts.com. These free software sites allow you to draw support and resistance zones, and use technical indicators you'll need when analyzing possible setups. We'll be talking more about technical analysis later in the book.

One more important consideration for you to consider is your broker's experience in dealing with options trading. You should be planning to expand your options trading knowledge and abilities, with The Wheel being just the start. One type of options trade that can be very profitable is the credit spread, where you enter 2 option legs at once. You already know what a spread is – you are effectively creating a spread trade when you roll that CC we discussed earlier. The more experienced brokers will allow you to enter both legs of your spread trades at once. This makes execution and capturing optimal prices much easier than entering each leg one at a time. It also insulates you from sudden bursts of market volatility.

CUSTOMER SERVICE QUALITY

This should go without saying, but you need to choose a broker with a high level of customer service. Unfortunately, these days, most customer service queries are handled by chatbots or an underpaid intern on Twitter. This is frustrating because you'll need to speak to a human every once in a while. Evaluating how quickly you can access a human being is an excellent metric to measure different brokers.

You can check this by typing a few questions into the chatbot software and then checking to see how soon the bot connects you through to a human. If it keeps you going round in circles, then it's a good indication that the company doesn't take customer support seriously enough. Many companies will ask you to leave your number and request a callback. This isn't good enough. If your situation is an emergency, you can hardly be expected to sit around waiting for a phone call from your broker.

Another way of evaluating their service is to send them an email and look at how long they take to get back to you. In most cases, the initial response will be quick. Send a follow-up question and wait for a response. By doing this, you're checking to see what kind of customer service process the company has. Most brokers figure that once initial questions are answered via email, the person asking them ends up opening an account. This leads them to not follow up on secondary emails.

The lack of response indicates poor after-sales service, and you should stay away from such brokers. The longer a broker has been in business, thebetter their customer service will be.

Choose a broker that has been around for a long time and read their reviews on impartial websites like Trustpilot. Always choose a broker that is registered with the Financial Regulatory Authority or FINRA. If you're juststarting out, avoid offshore brokers since all kinds of illegal and unethical behavior is possible with them.

OPTIONS ACCOUNT LEVEL REQUIREMENTS

To trade The Wheel in the U.S., you'll need to obtain approval from your broker, by completing a questionnaire about your investment experience, income, net worth and your trading plans.

Brokers typically have four or five option trading levels, with each successive one allowing more and more types of trades. Writing covered calls can typically be done with a Level 1 account. For cash secured puts though, many brokers require Level 2 account status. As you gain more knowledge about trading options, you will need to obtain a Level 3 or 4 approval to trade more sophisticated strategies.

Trading The Wheel in other countries becomes more complicated if your focus is on U.S. markets and stocks. You'll need to make sure your broker deals in international shares and you'll need to file Form W-8BEN with the

U.S. Internal Revenue Service. You'll also have to evaluate the additional fees that may be charged for international shares. The concept of option trading levels is also something to consider. You will need to ask your broker if CSPs are allowed with Level 1 or will you need Level 2 approval.

FEE SCHEDULE

In older times, many brokers could to get away with hiding fees within their fee schedules. This doesn't happen anymore, thanks to the increased transparency that strong competition has created. However, a few hidden fees still sneak in. For example, some brokers may charge an account maintenance fee every month if your total margin is less than $10,000. This isn't advertised as a minimum margin penalty, of course, so most people miss this fact.

There are other little fees that can add up. Wire transfer fees, account statement fees, dividend check payment and legal document fees can add up over time. A good broker will post a clear and easy to understand fee schedule on their website and will also mention it in their terms of service agreement that you'll sign when you open an account.

If the quality of the broker's software is glitchy and regularly stalls, you'll need to phone in your trades. Most brokers charge a fee for this, and it can be as high as $25 per trade. Inactivity charges are another way that brokers will make money off you. This is especially the case with brokers who seek active traders as customers. If you're transferring your balance from one broker to another, make sure you know if transfer fees apply. Quality brokers will not charge you for the incoming transfer.

These are the primary features of a broker that you must consider before choosing one. These days it's quite easy to read reviews of brokers and to figure out what their customers are saying about them. Take special note of the negative reviews. Not all of them will be legitimate, but an unusual number of reviews that mention the same problem is a good sign of something wrong with that broker.

TWO BROKERS WE RECOMMEND FOR THE WHEEL STRATEGY

Note: We are not affiliated with either of the companies listed below, nor do we receive any commissions if you open an account with them. Brokers andfees change all the time, so be sure to double check before you open an account

Tastyworks by Tastytrade

$1 per contract to open (capped at $10 per trade)
Cheaper fees for trading index options
Zero commissions to close
Can open/close both legs of the trade simultaneously
Easy to set up take automatic profit targets
Free ACH deposits & withdrawalsExcellent education platform Available to European users

Thinkorswim by TD Ameritrade

Commission free trading for US stocks & options
$0.65 per contract No assignment fees Easy to use softwareUS users only

"CAN I USE ROBINHOOD OR WEBULL FOR THIS?"

We get this question from email subscribers quite a lot, as many of them areusing Robinhood or WeBull to buy stocks.

The answer is... yes, but we don't recommend it.

Newer app-based solutions such as Robinhood and WeBull are a decent starting point for investing, but they're poor choices to execute the wheel with.

For starters, it's far better if you use a computer screen to execute these setups. This extra step of "inconvenience" also promotes rational thinking and reduces your propensity to make impulsive decisions. Combined with the fact that neither of these platforms has phone support if anything goes wrong (as you may have experienced with January's Gamestop fiasco) neither Robinhood nor WeBull is a good long term solution if you plan on executing The Wheel year round.

Chapter 4
CHOOSING THE RIGHT CANDIDATES

Now that you understand how The Wheel works, it's time to look at the stocks you should focus on to execute this strategy. On the surface, the criteria for selecting the right stocks is simple. Choose stocks you'd be happy to own for the long term, or ones that you'd be happy to run a covered call on.

However, there are many nuances to this, and we'll be covering these in thischapter. Always remember these overarching criteria when you read this chapter. Don't get caught up in speculative forces that will push you to implement The Wheel on hot stocks or fast-moving ones. How happy will you be owning a stock over the long term, is the fundamental question.

Will you be happy owning AT&T at $28 or Bank of America at $24? That'swhat you should always ask yourself before committing to run The Wheel on specific stocks. As a rule of thumb, if a stock is a good covered call candidate, it's likely to be a good one to run The Wheel on. The Wheel is anincome-generation strategy, but don't forget that price appreciation of the long stock will bring you the greatest gains over the long term.

If your focus is short term, then the premiums are what matter the most. You'll be better off writing options that are close to the money and capturing higher premiums in the process. When starting out, focus on your stock selection criteria more than anything else.

Selection Criteria

So, what are the criteria you should look for? There are a few different elements. Let's begin by examining the state of the stock overall.

Trend Characteristics

For The Wheel to work well you need to look for stocks that are either moving sideways in a range or slightly upwards. Stay away from stocks that are declining. Note that there is a difference between a stock that is declining slightly and one that is in freefall. It's a good idea to examine the stock chart for evidence of support and resistance levels before entering the trade. If you see relatively stable support and resistance levels within which prices are moving, this is evidence of a range or sideways move. We'll be explaining support and resistance and covering examples of this in the next chapter.

Stocks that move sideways allow you to capture higher premiums. This is because you can write options that are close to the money without the added risk of them being assigned. IV levels will also be lower and this means your trade will live in a stable environment. Of course, sideways moves cannot be sustained for long. At some point, the stock will break out, upwards or downwards, at which point you'll need to either adjust your strikes or decide whether you want your puts assigned and buy the stock.

A sharply declining stock is a poor candidate even if you want to own the stock. The reason being, the capital losses you'll face will override the premium income you earn. It's best to allow the stock to decline to lower levels and target a strong support level from which you can initiate thetrade.

A stock that is moving slightly upwards is a good candidate. However, note that these stocks can be more volatile and their IV numbers will reflect this. If you're happy owning it, consider writing your puts as close to the money as possible. If you'd like to earn additional income and enter when the uptrend is more defined, you can choose a strike that is further OTM.

If you aren't comfortable reading the price chart directly to determine what kind of a trend the stock is currently in, you can use indicators to help you figure this out. The ADX, for example, can help. This one is a trend strength indicator that fluctuates between 0 and 100, but it rarely hits those maximum values. Any number greater than 30 indicates a good trend, with numbers greater than 40 indicating a strong trend. Numbers below 30 indicate the absence of a trend. Good charting software will help you identify a stock's ADX value.

For The Wheel, you want to look for ADX numbers from 0 to 40, but if you're conservative, you can stick to values less than 30. Note that the ADX doesn't inform us about the direction of the trend, merely its strength. You'll need to look at the chart to figure out which way the stock is headed. A strong bearish trend will print the same numbers on the ADX as a strong bullish trend does.

You can also use moving averages and support/resistance analysis to help your evaluation of a stock's trend. We'll present some discussion and examples in the next chapter to help you better understand these analytics.

The internet is chock full of resources to help you grasp technical analysis and how to use it. If your grasp of the topic is weak, spend some time exploring the topic. Your trading results will improve as a result.

Stock Price

If your capital is low, you might be tempted to run The Wheel on low- priced or even penny stocks. The issue with this approach is that low-pricedstocks are extremely volatile and are just as likely to rise by a huge amount as they are to fall to the same degree. If you recall from the previoussection, you need to look at stocks that are in a moderate trend or are moving sideways.

These conditions almost never occur in stocks that are priced less than $5. If these stocks move sideways, it's because no one is trading them. Illiquidity is something you want to stay far away from. If the stock isn't being heavily traded, its options will suffer from even lower volumes. You'll find the premium spreads jumping all over the place and you'll have a hard time exiting your position.

By premium spread, we mean the difference between the bid and the ask. Typically you buy on the ask and sell on the bid. If the spread is wide, then, you may not get a price that makes the trade profitable. You'll find that the market in these low-priced stocks tends to be tilted towards one side. This means, even if the stock price rises, the spread just widens because the otherside of the market isn't present.

This is why many low-priced stocks move violently in either direction. For example, buyers pump the stock up to high levels and once they wish toexit, they find that the bid remains low. This means they exit at low prices and the price chart prints a violent correction.

Another issue with these low-priced stocks is most of them aren't traded on reputable exchanges. They're traded on OTC markets for the most part and their options are equally unreliable. It's therefore best to stay far away fromsub-$5 stocks. If you don't have the capital to trade stocks that are priced greater than this, then spend time acquiring enough capital to be able to do so. A lack of capital shouldn't push you towards trading unreliable stocks.

So how much capital do you need? With $2,000 you can trade one option ofa stock that's priced at $20, with $5,000 you can trade an ETF priced at $50, and with $10,000 you can trade an ETF or a stock priced at $100. You might think there aren't many low priced stocks for you to trade. However, this isn't true.

Bank of America, FLIR Systems, Coca-Cola, AT&T,

Intel and First Solar are examples of stocks that were good for people with smaller accounts in the past 2-3 years. With ETFs XLK (technology) and XLF (financials) weregood candidates.

These instruments have been moving within the same price range for a longtime now and are backed by decent fundamentals. This makes them great candidates for The Wheel. If you have access to a lot of capital, you can useit on higher priced stocks and ETFs like SPY & QQQ.

Stock Category

Well-known and recognized ETFs that are indexed. They could be indexed to a sector, an industry, or a popular market-tracking index. Whatever the underlying index is, make sure it's a nonvolatile one. The downside of participating in these ETFs is that they're often highly priced. However, we've highlighted a few exceptional ETFs that are moderately priced.

Look for ETFs that have been operational for at least 10 years and have a steady record of management. There shouldn't have been any mass chopping and changing of managers and the ETF should have posted returns closely in line with its index. The expense ratio should also be lowerthan 0.6% for a sector or thematic ETF and lower than 0.1% for a broad market or index ETF. Anything above this indicates fancy strategies thatyou ought to stay away from.

The assets under management (AUM) should be greater than $1 billion. This might sound like a lot of money, but for a reputable ETF with a good managerial team, it's pretty small. Most high-quality ETFs manage over

$10 billion or more. Think of the AUM as being the same as the stock price of a company. The greater it is, the better.

No IPOs

We could extend this piece of advice even for investment purposes as well. Stay away from IPOs, even if you believe the company in question is a slam dunk. As we'll explain shortly, a slam dunk is one of the worst candidates for The Wheel. The problem with IPOs is that they tend to be extremely volatile. Everyone in the market wants a piece of the action and the stock promoter wants to get as high a price for their stock as possible.

Remember that companies raise cash from IPOs. For this reason, IPO pricestend to be inflated. As the market recognizes what's going on, violent corrections are possible. This is why the implied volatility of IPO stocks tends to be quite high. While volatility will help you on occasion, relying on it to produce consistent results isn't an intelligent decision.

Often, investors jump into IPOs because they buy the hype surrounding these companies. Stay well away from them and you'll do yourself a huge favor.

Stick to Boring Companies

High-growth companies are stock market darlings because they deliver astronomical returns quicker than a regular company's stock does. A portfolio of one or two high-growth stocks should be more than enough for you to be able to retire comfortably. For example, anyone who bought Amazon back in 2011 or earlier is probably sitting on a decent nest egg right now. Apple is also an example of a high-growth stock.

You'd think that capturing income as well as large capital gains will boost an already lucrative investment, and therefore The Wheel would be well suited for these companies. However, when you try to execute The Wheel on these stocks in real life, you'll find yourself leaving a ton of money on the table.

Thanks to the rapid appreciation that these company's stocks can undergo, your CSP is unlikely to move ITM. This means you won't be buying the stock. Even if you do manage to buy it, there's the problem of selecting a CC's strike price. If your CC finishes in the money and the stock is called away, you've capped your profit, thereby limiting your upside gains on these stocks.

Remember that the stock leg is the primary driver of gains. The option legs provide you with income that augments these primary gains. If a growth stock is primed to rise by 100% annually, it doesn't make sense to give this up in exchange for income that amounts to a one or two percent gain.

This theory was put to the test on Apple's stock by quantitative research firm Spintwig ("AAPL Short Put 45 DTE Cash-Secured Options Backtest," 2019). As a part of this backtest, 31,700 trades were placed on Apple over a 10-year period from 2008 to 2018. The options that were written in this test had an average expiration range of 45 days. This meant the strategy captured time decay in its entirety. This is another way of saying that the option premiums were maximized.

Positions in this backtest were managed early and often to adjust for optimum strike prices and this increased the average daily P/L per position from twice to 3.67x. The results of this backtest were great.

However, when the results were compared to a simple buy and hold strategy on the stock over the same time period, the options strategy underperformed massively.

This is because the rise in Apple's stock price was astronomical. There's no way option premiums can ever make up for a fast-rising stock price. This is why we counsel against operating The Wheel on stocks that you believe are likely to be home runs. If you spot any stock that you believe will be the next Apple or Amazon, then it's best to buy it outright and hold on to it for as long as possible. Don't bother writing options on it and risk it beingtaken from you during exercise.

You don't want to give up your long position in exchange for a few pointsin premiums. When viewed from a convenience perspective, it's hard to seewhy you would want to write options on these stocks. You'll have to spend time worrying about losing a good position and have to constantly watchout for vertical moves in the stock that could move your calls ITM.

It's better to stick to boring stocks that don't move much and won't giveyou sleepless nights. Going back to our earlier baseball analogy, don'tbother trying to hit home runs. Stick to hitting singles and doubles instead. You'll compound these gains more reliably over the long term. If you hit upon a high-growth stock, buy it and plan to hold it long term.

To really drive the point home, let's answer the question one of our readers put to us recently: Is implementing The Wheel on Amazon stock a good idea or not. We say it's not a good idea, and recommended a buy and hold strategy for the following reasons.

First, to buy 100 shares of Amazon, the reader would need $320,000 incash. This amount secures the CSP. There's also the fact that premiums on Amazon options are quite low. You're not going to earn much. Even with a

0.3 Delta (we'll explain Deltas in a later chapter if you're not familiar with them) you're going to earn just 4% per month, if that. Add to this the time you'll need to spend monitoring the trade, in case your CC moves ITM, andthe strategy is already looking like it isn't worth it.

Most damning of all, the opportunity cost of having over $300,000 lockedin a single trade is enormous, unless your portfolio is worth more than $30 million. Your profit, from running The Wheel on Amazon, will yield around 40% annually. This is great and outstrips the 18% you can earn by runningit on the SPY. (Note that this is using 2020 numbers, so it is an analysis of the past - not a prediction.)

However in 2020, a simple buy and hold on Amazon yielded 73.5%, whilea buy and hold approach on the SPY, on average, will yield 13%. Thelesson here is that it's worth running The Wheel on the SPY, if you have thecash, but on Amazon you're simply creating more headaches for yourself by limiting your upside potential.

One way to mitigate this temptation is to apply a 1% dividend yield filter when screening for potential stocks. This will remove all growth stocksfrom your final list.

No Media Darlings

The financial media loves talking up certain companies as the "next Apple/Amazon/Facebook," etc. Often new sectors spring to life and this leads to a gold rush within those stocks. Over the previous decade, sectors such as marijuana and electric vehicles boomed and made some investors a fortune. However, we're willing to bet there were a greater number of investors who lost money in these companies.

Marijuana was the first darling of the decade. With promises of alternative medicine and the scientific proof that established cannabis and cannabinoids as legitimate healing methods, many companies rushed into the field once it was legalized. There were secondary effects of this boom as well. Virtually everyone who could grow marijuana became a "farmer" and sought to cash in on the boom.

In the stock market, companies that operated so-called weed farms became hot and zoomed in value. A few years later, most of these companies fell right back down because the economics of the sector didn't support valuations. We're not saying you shouldn't invest in this sector. It's just that every company that the media hypes ends up being a terrible long-term investment.

Media hype fuels price rises because everyone jumps into the stock. The electric vehicle sector is a good case in point. Tesla has been the flag-bearer for EV companies for a long time now. Many of its competitors have gone bankrupt trying to make the terrible economics of the sector work for them. However, thanks to smart capital raising, Tesla has operated like a tech startup, burning cash all the time, hoping to gain enough customers to buy their vehicles.

Other EV companies have jumped into the fray, using Special Purpose Acquisition Companies or SPACs to avoid having to go through the IPO process and the scrutiny that comes with it. Many Chinese companies that used to manufacture CDs are now EV makers. A graduate in mechanical engineering from Carnegie Mellon University founded an EV company and became a billionaire despite laughable revenue projections and zero technology.

Our point is that these hot sectors eventually come crashing back down. You'll be left holding the bag when this happens and your option premium income isn't going to be of any consolation. If capital gains are the primary profit driver, then capital losses are the primary loss driver. The quality of the company whose stock you're planning on holding matters more than anything else.

Some of the things to watch out for are companies that are dubbed the "next [insert favorite stock]". This kind of marketing panders to the get-rich-quick crowd that doesn't bother researching the companies they put their money into. Follow them and you'll receive their results. The next thing to look out for is a company that is clearly cashing in on the speculative hype around it.

The other kind of media darling to watch out for is the institutional darling. These companies are favored by large hedge funds and find themselves in the news because some money manager goes on air and starts talking about it. We're not saying that their motives are malicious. However, these companies always see a boost in their stock price in the short term before settling down.

Ultimately, all the media does is increase volatility in a stock. Because high volatility is your enemy when implementing The Wheel, you want to stay as far away as possible from it. Pick boring stocks that have boring businesses and you'll earn steady returns from them through their option premiums. With high-growth companies, such as Amazon or Apple, buy their stocks outright and don't bother with generating income from their options.

No Penny Stocks

We've already mentioned that the stocks you select need to trade for at least

$5, or maybe even $10. However, we'll make special mention of penny stocks because many novice investors tend to be tempted by them at some point. Penny stocks are a bad idea no matter which angle you examine them from.

The standard narrative around a penny stock investment is that you can buy a stock for a few cents and see it rise to a few dollars. This rise will give you a four-digit return (in percentage terms). Gaining this much in blue chip stocks is impossible. After all, even a 100% rise in Amazon would put its stock price at around $6,500. The other factor to consider is that Amazon is already a trillion-dollar company. Doubling this is a considerable task.

Penny stock companies are typically worth a few hundred million or less. It's easier for a company to double a market cap of $100 million or less. This situation attracts many fortune hunters. However, despite their wish to act like investors, everyone ends up behaving like a speculator. The volatility in penny stocks forces them to behave like this.

Swings of 50% or more over a week aren't uncommon in penny stocks. Consider that a stock that sells for 50 cents has moved by 100% if it sells for a dollar. The numerical price doesn't seem too much, but its effect on your portfolio will be substantial. Many investors lose their nerve and end up trying to time their entries and exits. Even worse, some traders use leverage to boost their returns.

What happens instead is that they lose their shirts. Volatility is the reason you should stay away from penny stocks. Most of these stocks don't have active disclosure requirements because they aren't listed on the stock exchange. As we mentioned previously, they trade over the counter and their volumes are minimal. You'll be operating against company insiders who don't have insider trader laws to worry about. It's a lose-lose situation for you no matter which way you cut it.

You'll read many stories from trading gurus about how they turned a few thousands into millions using penny stocks. Some of them might even be former "hedge fund" principals. Take these stories with a truckload of salt.

When former hedge fund managers sell courses to make a living, they were probably not very good at what they did.

So, stay away from anything to do with penny stocks or the people whopush them.

Specialty ETFs

Leveraged ETFs are the penny stocks of the investment fund world. We briefly mentioned these previously, but it's time to dive deeper into them. There are different kinds of leveraged ETFs you'll find in the markets. The first kind are the plain vanilla leveraged ETFs. TQQQ and TNA are examples of this category.

TQQQ aims to earn three times the returns of any movement on the NASDAQ. If the NASDAQ moves by a point, TQQQ moves by three. The way it does this is by borrowing money, thereby leveraging itself. TNAaims to 3X small-cap stock index returns. Small-caps tend to outperform large-caps in the long run. However, they do so with greater volatility.

To 3X these returns sounds like a great idea on paper. After all, most indexes rise over the long term and it isn't as if the NASDAQ is going to disappear anytime soon. So why not buy and hold a leveraged ETF overthat time period? The problem with this line of thinking is that it doesn't take volatility into account. You cannot hold on to something for the long term if short-term volatility forces you into a margin call caused by amarket correction.

These ETFs haven't faced such a situation as yet, but it's not an implausibleone. If the market dips, these

ETFs dip by 3X thanks to leverage. That's the price you pay for investing in them. Devoting a small portion of your portfolio to them might be a good move, as long as you understand the risk, but when it comes to implementing The Wheel on these ETFs, you need to reconsider your choice.

Excessive volatility will push prices in unpredictable ways. You might find that your CSP is ITM for the large majority of the holding period, but it moves OTM at the last minute. Using The Wheel on volatile instruments is like riding a rollercoaster. It's great for a few short minutes, but no one wants to be on it for a long time.

There's another category of leveraged ETFs you should stay away from. These are inverse ETFS that move in the opposite direction from their underlying index. The way they do this is by assuming short positions in the index using options. Implementing The Wheel on these ETFs is a risky move. Effectively, you'll be opening an option position on another option.

A single option position leverages your investment considerably since you'll control 100 shares of the underlying. To double this exposure isn't a smart move. Add to this mix the inherent volatility that these ETFs have and you've created a very risky situation. Stay away from inverse ETFs.

Many ETFs track commodities, and these can seem like a good option. Commodity investing is a diverse field and there are many ways that ETF managers can track their underlying product. Some choose the plain vanilla way by tracking index prices. Others track it by buying stocks in companies that have exposure to the commodity. Then there are the adventurous ones who track prices by buying futures and speculating on prices.

These too are especially risky. USO, which aims to track oil prices, is a good example. This ETF derives its price by speculating on WTI futures. However, when oil prices went negative in 2020 thanks to the COVID-19 crisis, the managers of USO changed their strategy without any notice and this caused the ETF's price to plummet even as oil prices were rebounding. Finally, we have ETFs that track volatility. UVXY is an example of this. This ETF derives its prices from the VIX and offers a direct path to betting on volatility. There are many problems with investing in such complicated ETFs. Volatility is a derivative of the market. It measures how fast prices are moving, not their direction.

To make an intelligent guess about volatility, you need to be able to read market conditions extremely well and this takes time. It certainly isn'tsomething you can do if you have only a few hours per week to devote to market analysis. Expert institutional investors get volatility investing wrong, so it's unrealistic to assume you can figure it out by spending a few hours per week.

The lesson here is that commodity ETFs or ETFs that don't directly track a simple index of stocks are a risky bet. They're volatile, and as an investor, you're at the fund manager's mercy. There's no telling when they might change their approach and leave you holding the bag.

Implementing The Wheel on these ETFs adds another layer of derivatives onto the situation. There's no telling how prices will move, and adjusting your position is going to be extremely tricky. It's best to stay away from them altogether.

STOCK SCREENER CRITERIA

To make stock selection easier, we recommend using a stock screener to help you narrow down your investment choices. There are a number of screening tools and sites, ranging from free to extremely expensive.

Finviz is perhaps the best free stock screener out there because it allows you to input both fundamental and technical criteria. Based on what we've said thus far in this chapter, here is the criteria you can input into Finviz to find stocks which tick our required boxes. Try accessing Finviz.com now and follow along as we tell you exactly what filters to select. Near the top of the page, you should see a horizontal ribbon with the word "Screener" in it. Click on it and make sure "All" filters is selected.

Optionality

To execute The Wheel, we need stocks that we are eligible to write options on, so find the Option filter and make sure Optionable is selected.

Price

Next, we fix our price criteria. Let's focus on $10 per

share. The maximum price depends on your capital, because you will need enough money in youraccount to buy 100 shares when you take assignment of your CSP. So if your capital is $5,000 then your maximum price per share is $50.

Volume

Next, you should stick to stocks and ETFs that are heavily traded. Choosean average daily volume of at least 200,000 shares - with the last session's ("Current volume") equal to or greater than this number. This will weed outall instruments that are thinly traded as well as the ones that had volume spikes distort the average volume.

Stability

Filtering out growth stocks is important. Add a filter for a one-percent dividend yield and you'll get rid of high-growth stocks. These companies rarely pay dividends, which is why this filter works. Note that it isn'tperfect. You'll need to check your list to check whether there are any mediadarlings in there.

Bullish Trend

Another good filter has price greater than the 50 Exponential Moving Average. Your version of Finviz may only offer the simple moving average as a filter. That's fine – use it if necessary. By screening for stocks above the 50 moving average, you will be identifying stocks in moderate bull trends. Of course, any stock could swing downwards violently once you enter, but this is a risk you'll have to assume. Technical analysis will help to screen stocks, as well. We'll cover that in the next chapter.

No Upcoming Events

One of the most important filters you should include is requiring that there are no earnings announcements coming up over the next 30 days. For the Earnings Date filter, chose "Previous Week". Many beginner options traders fall into the trap of writing options during earnings week. The thought process is that earnings week implies higher volatility, which means greater IV levels. This boosts premiums and therefore writing a CSP is a good idea. However, higher IVs also imply a greater potential drop in prices, even if the earnings exceed expectations.

Earnings announcements usually are not a major mover of stock prices; the earnings expected are already factored into prices. This doesn't happen because of insider information. Instead, Wall Street analysts gain deep access into the company's inner workings and project an earnings rate that is in line with the company's internal expectations.

This number forms a "baseline" for companies to hit and you typically do not see earnings reported much below or above this number. Thus, stock prices normally reflect earnings projections and the news is built into the price. The Covid-19 crisis, however, has shown how earnings projections can be wrong, and how stock prices can move violently in reaction. Therefore, you are better avoiding the stock price fluctuation that can occur with earnings surprises.

ETFs have an advantage in this regard. There are no earnings to report even if the underlying stocks report earnings. If you're sticking to ETFs, you won't have to worry about applying this filter.

				Descriptive(7)	Fundamental	Technical(1)	All(8)				

Exchange	Any	Index	Any	Sector	Any	Industry	Any	Country	USA
Market Cap.	+Mid (over $2B)	Dividend Yield	Over 1%	Float Short	Any	Analyst Recom.	Any	Option/Short	Optionable
Earnings Date	Previous Week	Average Volume	Over 200K	Relative Volume	Any	Current Volume	Any	Price	Under $50
Target Price	Any	IPO Date	Any	Shares Outstanding	Any	Float	Any		Reset (0)

Overview | Valuation | Financial | Ownership | Performance | Technical | Custom | Charts | Tickers | Basic | TA | News | Snapshot | Stats

No.	Ticker	Company	Sector	Industry	Country	Market Cap	P/E	Price	Change	Volume
1	AEO	American Eagle Outfitters, Inc.	Consumer Cyclical	Apparel Retail	USA	4.89B	20.01	1.56%	3,006,331
2	BGS	B&G Foods, Inc.	Consumer Defensive	Packaged Foods	USA	2.09B	15.76	22.11	0.72%	1,421,747
3	FSK	FS KKR Capital Corp.	Financial	Asset Management	USA	2.54B	20.96	1.19%	602,806
4	FSKR	FS KKR Capital Corp. II	Financial	Asset Management	USA	3.40B	20.00	1.47%	615,240
5	GPS	The Gap, Inc.	Consumer Cyclical	Apparel Retail	USA	11.16B	30.91	1.32%	8,741,159
6	HPE	Hewlett Packard Enterprise Company	Technology	Communication Equipment	USA	20.17B	15.61	1.69%	14,172,274
7	KR	The Kroger Co.	Consumer Defensive	Grocery Stores	USA	26.60B	10.64	33.40	1.49%	10,701,926
8	NRG	NRG Energy, Inc.	Utilities	Utilities - Independent Power Producers	USA	10.41B	20.15	41.59	2.49%	3,147,957
9	TCDA	TECDA Inc.	Communication Services	Broadcasting	USA	4.30B	9.04	19.69	0.51%	1,245,465

Figure 2: *The Finviz screening criteria taken on March 14th 2021. As you can see, using the above criteria we have a selection of 8 stocks which would potentially be good candidates for The Wheel if your account size was less than $5,000.*

Paid Screening Tools

Aside from Finviz.com, you can use Barchart.com. The free version of barchart.com is quite robust, and the premium version contains a few criteria that are useful. The premium version costs $200 per year and allows you to screen stocks based on their IV level. IV is directly tied to option prices: the higher the IV, the higher the price of the option. As an option seller, we want to earn higher premiums, but doing so comes at a risk. The reason premiums are higher is because volatility is higher, and our stock has a potentially bigger range of movement during the option contract's lifespan.

Therefore when looking at IV level, we like to use the sweet spot of an IV between 30 and 50%.

So stay away from stocks like AMC that have a 408% IV number.

General Motors (40%), Twitter (39%), AMD (37%) Fox Corporation (36%), are more suitable Wheel candidates.

Barcharts premium version also allows you to select custom earnings dates, as Figure 3 illustrates.

Figure 3: *Barchart.com Paid Screener*

This concludes our look at the fundamental criteria for choosing stocks toimplement The Wheel with. As you can see, they're quite straightforward, and they're extremely powerful. Not only are fundamental filters such as the ones we've highlighted, great, so are technical filters.

Technical analysis is often overlooked by long-term investors, but in our opinion, it has the potential to improve your ability to choose good candidates for The Wheel. The next chapter deals with technical analysis as it relates to screening stocks for The Wheel.

CPSIA information can be obtained
at www.ICGtesting.com
Printed in the USA
BVHW031141090822
644144BV00016B/831